Practice Test 2
for the CogAT® - Form 7

Cognitive Abilities Test®
Level 9 (Grade 3)

By Smart Cookie Ink

COPYRIGHT 2017

Printed in the United States of America.

INTRODUCTION

The *Cognitive Abilities Test®* (*CogAT®*) measures a student's reasoning and problem solving abilities using Verbal, Quantitative and Figurative approaches.

This test is administered to K–12 school children as a means to identify potentially gifted children for placement in accelerated learning programs. A good score on the CogAT® qualifies a child for superior educational programs within public and private schools.

Analytical reasoning and problem solving are seldom part of the standard school curriculum. Most children appear for the CogAT® without a clear understanding of what is expected of them. Sometimes even the brightest of young minds can be rattled because of unfamiliarity with the questions and test format.   They are forced to respond reflexively in the absence of a test taking strategy.

Schools suggest a good night's sleep and a healthy breakfast as adequate preparation – as well-intended as this advice may be, it just won't cut it in this increasingly competitive environment.

Help your child perform at his or her best AND ensure that his or her true potential is fairly and accurately evaluated!

With this in mind, we have designed this book with a specific purpose: to hone your child's analytical reasoning and problem solving abilities that the Grade 3 CogAT® test demands.

This book covers one full length Level 9 test for Grade 3 students.

The practice test that this book offers will
➢   Help tune your child's mind to think critically
➢   Provide varied exercises in all the areas of reasoning that the test considers:

   • **Verbal**
   (Verbal Analogies, Sentence Completion & Verbal Classification)
   • **Quantitative**
   (Number Analogies, Number Puzzles & Number Series)
   • **Figurative**
   (Figure Matrices, Paper Folding & Figure Classification)

➢   Familiarize your child with the format of the test.
In addition, the book also offers,
➢   Important test taking tips and strategies

Now, get ready to ace this test!

TABLE OF CONTENTS

TIPS FOR THE TESTERS

• A GOOD NIGHT'S SLEEP & A HEALTHY BREAKFAST!

The test is spread over 2 to 5 days in most school districts. Make sure you get a good night's sleep and eat a healthy breakfast and arrive to school on time on these important days of testing. A calm mind is usually able to think significantly better!

• I said "LISTEN!"

Listen to the instructions given to you during the examination. You will be given instructions on how to fill the test forms. Be sure to follow these instructions. You do not want to compromise your test score because you filled in the answers incorrectly or in the wrong section!

As you already may know, the CogAT® test is divided into multiple sections. You will be provided with directions at the start of each section. The directions will explain the section and tell you how the questions in it should be answered. Pay attention even though you may be familiar with the test format.

Sometimes, the questions within each section may be read to you instead of it being provided in written form. If the questions are being read to you, please focus and listen carefully! They will not be repeated. It is important that you pay close attention to the reversing effect of negative words (like not) or prefixes (like un-).

• WHAT IS IN YOUR MIND'S EYE?

Before looking at the answers, it might help if you try to first solve the question in your mind. This approach works well especially for Quantitative sections.

<Cont'd>

• EVALUATE ALL ANSWER CHOICES!

Evaluate all answer choices and always choose the one right answer which BEST answers the question. Remember, sometimes the best available answer might not be the most ideal answer or the answer in your mind's eye. You are just choosing the best of the lot!

• SLASH THE TRASH!

If you can eliminate one or two obviously wrong answer choices at the first glance, you can focus on picking the correct answer from among the remaining choices.

• TAKE A GUESS!

CogAT® test scores are calculated based on the number of right answers. It is best to answer all questions rather than leave them blank. If after 'slashing the trash', you do not know the correct answer, guess from the available 'maybe' answers.

• COLOR THE BUBBLE!

It is important to know how to color the bubble. Sometimes, you may be given a bubble test form. At other times, you may have to color the bubbles just below the answer choices within the question paper. Practice coloring bubbles and using a sample bubble test form. Also, remember to color only one bubble per question.

In the recent years, some schools have chosen to administer the test on a computer or tablet. This is not common and depends on your individual school district. In the event the test is paperless, students typically go through a sample test at school before the actual test to familiarize themselves with the common and intuitive user interface. (For example, 'forward arrow' or 'next' button to go to the next question; 'backward arrow' to go the previous question etc).

Practice Test 2
for the CogAT® - Form 7

Cognitive Abilities Test®

Level 9 (Grade 3)

VERBAL ANALOGIES

In each question, find the relationship between the first two words. Pick the word that has the same relationship when paired with the third word. Color the bubble under your choice.

1. **plant : seed :: flower :**

   ⓐ twig ⓑ bud ⓒ thorn ⓓ leaf ⓔ rose

2. **summer : season :: December :**

   ⓐ month ⓑ Christmas ⓒ year ⓓ winter ⓔ snow

3. **dough : bread :: batter :**

   ⓐ baking ⓑ pancake ⓒ oven ⓓ flour ⓔ icing

4. **bee : hive :: rabbit :**

   ⓐ burrow ⓑ condo ⓒ nest ⓓ den ⓔ coop

5. **coffee : beans :: tea :**

   ⓐ milk ⓑ cup ⓒ leaves ⓓ drink ⓔ sugar

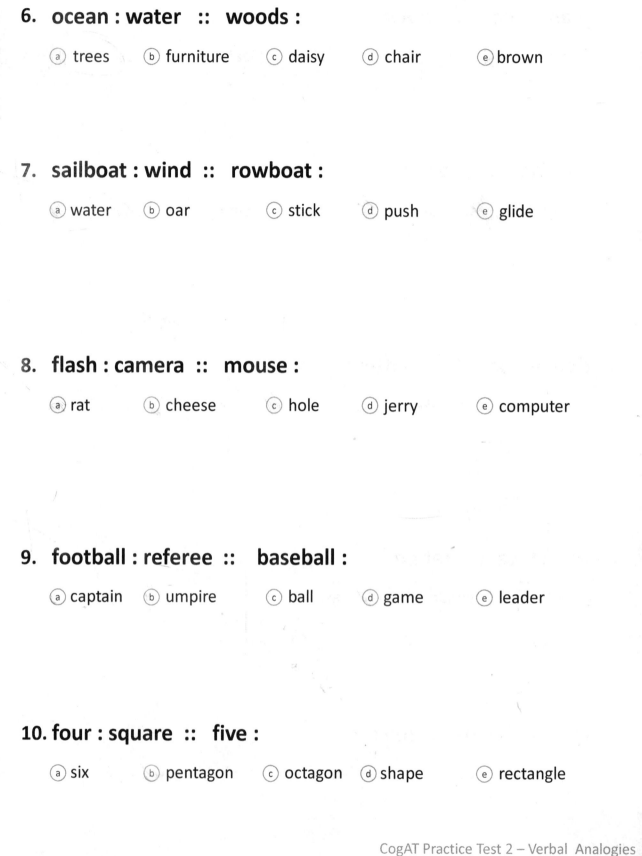

6. ocean : water :: woods :

  (a) trees   (b) furniture   (c) daisy   (d) chair   (e) brown

7. sailboat : wind :: rowboat :

  (a) water   (b) oar   (c) stick   (d) push   (e) glide

8. flash : camera :: mouse :

  (a) rat   (b) cheese   (c) hole   (d) jerry   (e) computer

9. football : referee :: baseball :

  (a) captain   (b) umpire   (c) ball   (d) game   (e) leader

10. four : square :: five :

  (a) six   (b) pentagon   (c) octagon   (d) shape   (e) rectangle

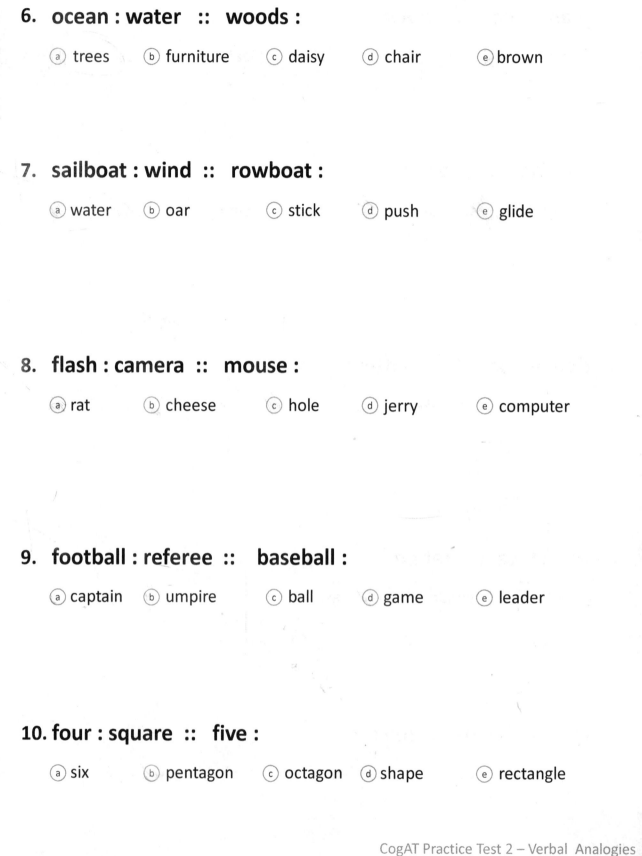

11. snake : slither :: lion :

     (a) hunt   (b) prowl   (c) hop   (d) attack   (e) waddle

12. pilot : plane :: captain :

     (a) sports   (b) sea   (c) ship   (d) bus   (e) helicopter

13. nut : shell :: pea :

     (a) cover   (b) soup   (c) plant   (d) pod   (e) vegetable

14. run : ran :: sink :

     (a) float   (b) sanked   (c) sank   (d) sunked   (e) sinked

15. belt : waist :: bracelet :

     (a) wrist   (b) neck   (c) arm   (d) gold   (e) jewelry

16. rain : flood :: snow :

    ⓐ winter   ⓑ flakes   ⓒ wind   ⓓ blizzard   ⓔ tornado

17. teacher : teach :: doctor :

    ⓐ clinic   ⓑ medicine   ⓒ treat   ⓓ patient   ⓔ nurse

18. cub : bear :: joey :

    ⓐ happy   ⓑ kangaroo   ⓒ toy   ⓓ lion   ⓔ elephant

19. fern : plant :: eel :

    ⓐ fish   ⓑ game   ⓒ tree   ⓓ bird   ⓔ mammal

20. puppies : litter :: fish :

    ⓐ group   ⓑ gang   ⓒ herd   ⓓ band   ⓔ school

21. cat : kitten :: cow :

    ⓐ baby   ⓑ buffalo   ⓒ cub   ⓓ sibling   ⓔ calf

22. scientist : experiment :: actor :

    ⓐ lab   ⓑ play   ⓒ game   ⓓ swim   ⓔ husband

23. diamond : baseball :: court :

    ⓐ tennis   ⓑ poker   ⓒ park   ⓓ swimming   ⓔ jury

24. Continent : Asia :: Planet :

    ⓐ Sun   ⓑ Martian   ⓒ Jupiter   ⓓ Life   ⓔ Stars

SENTENCE COMPLETION

Each question in this section has a sentence that is missing a word. Pick the word that **BEST** completes the sentence by coloring the bubble under it.

1. Susan _____ into the swimming pool, splashing water everywhere!

   ⓐ swam   ⓑ plunged   ⓒ bent   ⓓ climbed   ⓔ stepped

2. I helped my dad _____ tomatoes in our vegetable garden yesterday.

   ⓐ grow   ⓑ plant   ⓒ try   ⓓ prepare   ⓔ throw

3. The dog broke into a frenzied run and _____ over the tall fence.

   ⓐ leaped   ⓑ climbed   ⓒ ran   ⓓ walked   ⓔ jumping

4. My sister _____ the flowers in the vase beautifully.

   ⓐ cut   ⓑ threw   ⓒ puts   ⓓ left   ⓔ arranged

5. Although James was _____, he performed wonderfully.

   ⓐ jealous   ⓑ pleased   ⓒ nervous   ⓓ overjoyed   ⓔ confident

6. **Our teacher helped us find a _____ to the problem.**

   ⓐ book   ⓑ puzzle   ⓒ solution   ⓓ question   ⓔ answer

7. **The oven is very hot! Be careful not to _____ your hands!**

   ⓐ hurt   ⓑ sting   ⓒ cut   ⓓ bruise   ⓔ burn

8. **My Science teacher let me _____ the seed under a microscope.**

   ⓐ touch   ⓑ examine   ⓒ try   ⓓ water   ⓔ pot

9. **Amy is _____ than her mother already!**

   ⓐ tallest   ⓑ taller   ⓒ tall   ⓓ shortest   ⓔ shorter

10. **Honeybees drink _____ from flowers.**

    ⓐ nectar   ⓑ water   ⓒ juice   ⓓ honey   ⓔ liquid

11. **We decided to take _____ of the good weather and go for a walk.**

   ⓐ leave   ⓑ in   ⓒ over   ⓓ relief   ⓔ advantage

12. **I wasn't allowed into the cinema hall because I had lost my _____.**

   ⓐ card   ⓑ money   ⓒ wallet   ⓓ ticket   ⓔ friend

13. **We cancelled the picnic _____ it started raining.**

   ⓐ if   ⓑ because   ⓒ so   ⓓ and   ⓔ but

14. **We saw a _____ of cows grazing the field below.**

   ⓐ group   ⓑ bunch   ⓒ flock   ⓓ batch   ⓔ herd

15. **The medicines helped Janet _____ quickly.**

   ⓐ recover   ⓑ read   ⓒ talk   ⓓ snore   ⓔ test

16. Raymond cooks wonderful Italian food. We _____ the pasta dish he made for lunch.

ⓐ disliked ⓑ helped ⓒ enjoyed ⓓ likes ⓔ eating

17. Michele and Mike sat under a tree _____ the lake and decided to wait for their friends.

ⓐ to ⓑ through ⓒ on ⓓ in ⓔ by

18. Elizabeth, please hurry! I am certain that the train _____ at 3:30 p.m.

ⓐ goes ⓑ leaving ⓒ leave ⓓ leaves ⓔ gone

19. I am very fond _____ country music.

ⓐ with ⓑ over ⓒ of ⓓ in ⓔ at

20. Rupert _____ his troubles bravely.

ⓐ tried ⓑ did ⓒ wished ⓓ created ⓔ faced

VERBAL CLASSIFICATION

Each question in this section has a set of 3 words on the top. Determine how they are similar. Pick the one answer choice that is most similar to the top 3. Color the bubble next to your choice.

Note : Be sure to pick an answer that is similar to the top three words, NOT a word that describes them.

1. **butter   cheese   cream**
   ⓐ bread   ⓑ yogurt   ⓒ pie   ⓓ jam   ⓔ eggs

2. **ship   submarine   steamer**
   ⓐ car   ⓑ boat   ⓒ bus   ⓓ wheel   ⓔ airplane

3. **potato   beetroot   turnip**
   ⓐ carrot   ⓑ cabbage   ⓒ soup   ⓓ spinach   ⓔ vegetables

4. **bleat   neigh   grunt**
   ⓐ joke   ⓑ sob   ⓒ yell   ⓓ argue   ⓔ roar

5. **camellia   poppy   sunflower**
   ⓐ apple   ⓑ plant   ⓒ leaves   ⓓ magnolia   ⓔ flower

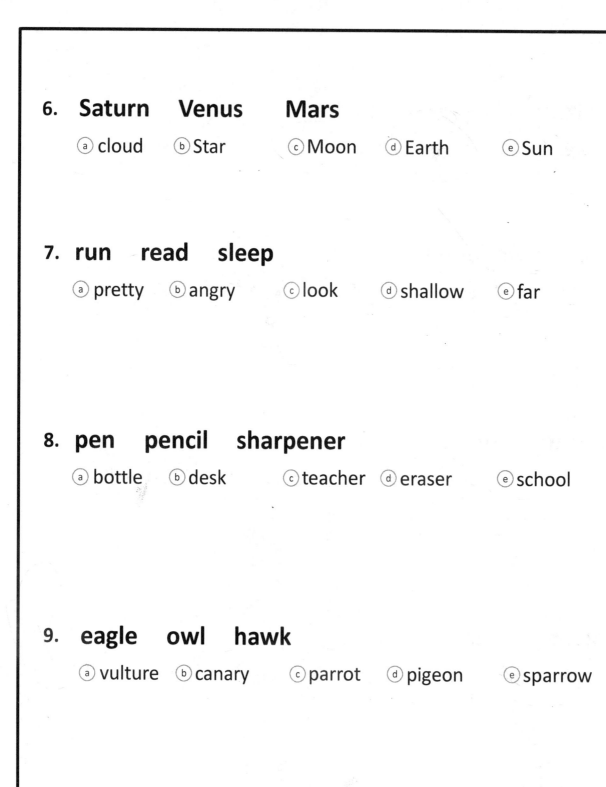

6. Saturn   Venus   Mars

ⓐ cloud   ⓑ Star   ⓒ Moon   ⓓ Earth   ⓔ Sun

7. run   read   sleep

ⓐ pretty   ⓑ angry   ⓒ look   ⓓ shallow   ⓔ far

8. pen   pencil   sharpener

ⓐ bottle   ⓑ desk   ⓒ teacher   ⓓ eraser   ⓔ school

9. eagle   owl   hawk

ⓐ vulture   ⓑ canary   ⓒ parrot   ⓓ pigeon   ⓔ sparrow

10. whale   walrus   dolphin

ⓐ worm   ⓑ seal   ⓒ snake   ⓓ crab   ⓔ crocodile

11. almond   cashew walnut

    ⓐ nuts   ⓑ chocolate   ⓒ butter   ⓓ bean   ⓔ macadamia

12. bison   ram   rhinoceros

    ⓐ tiger   ⓑ antelope   ⓒ hippo   ⓓ giraffe   ⓔ flounder

13. cake   ice-cream   pie

    ⓐ mousse   ⓑ burger   ⓒ pizza   ⓓ corn   ⓔ meat-loaf

14. plane   helicopter   rocket

    ⓐ fan   ⓑ scooter   ⓒ jet   ⓓ car   ⓔ kite

15. strong   brave   round

    ⓐ laugh   ⓑ play   ⓒ cry   ⓓ sharp   ⓔ shout

16. pilot   teacher   doctor

    ⓐ college   ⓑ degree   ⓒ patient   ⓓ clerk   ⓔ archipelago

17. lake   river   stream

    ⓐ sea   ⓑ ocean   ⓒ beach   ⓓ pond   ⓔ rain

18. Christmas   Halloween   New Year

    ⓐ Winter   ⓑ Easter   ⓒ Holiday   ⓓ Santa   ⓔ Birthday

19. ring   bracelet   earing

    ⓐ tie   ⓑ gold   ⓒ jewelry   ⓓ bangle   ⓔ mascara

20. golf   soccer   baseball

    ⓐ chess   ⓑ bowling   ⓒ cards   ⓓ football   ⓔ monopoly

NUMBER ANALOGIES

In each question, find the relationship between the first two sets of numbers. Pick a number that has the same relationship when paired with the number in the third set. Color the bubble under your choice.

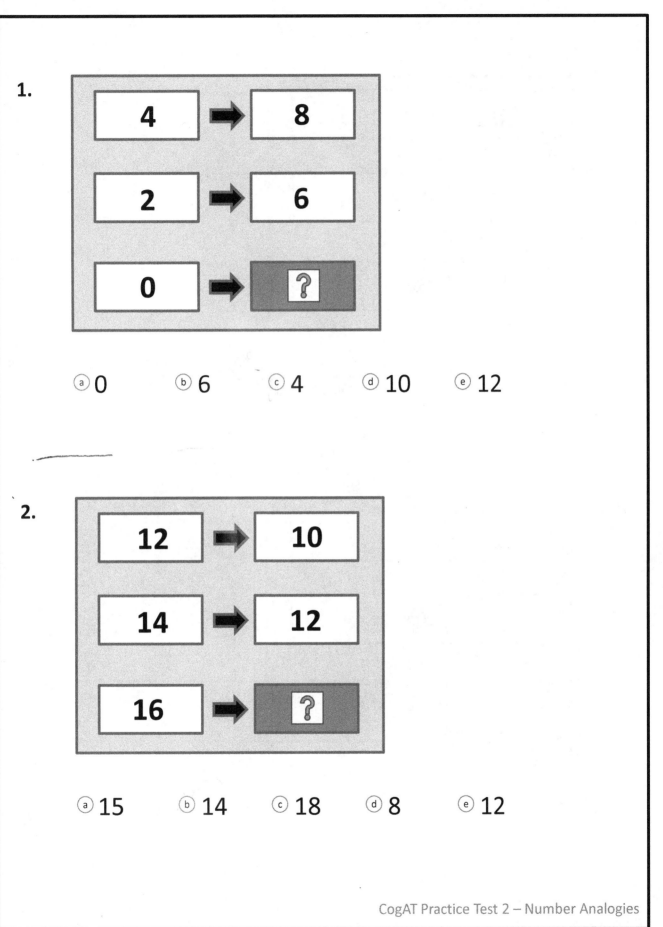

1.

4 ➡	**8**
2 ➡	**6**
0 ➡	**?**

ⓐ 0   ⓑ 6   ⓒ 4   ⓓ 10   ⓔ 12

2.

12 ➡	**10**
14 ➡	**12**
16 ➡	**?**

ⓐ 15   ⓑ 14   ⓒ 18   ⓓ 8   ⓔ 12

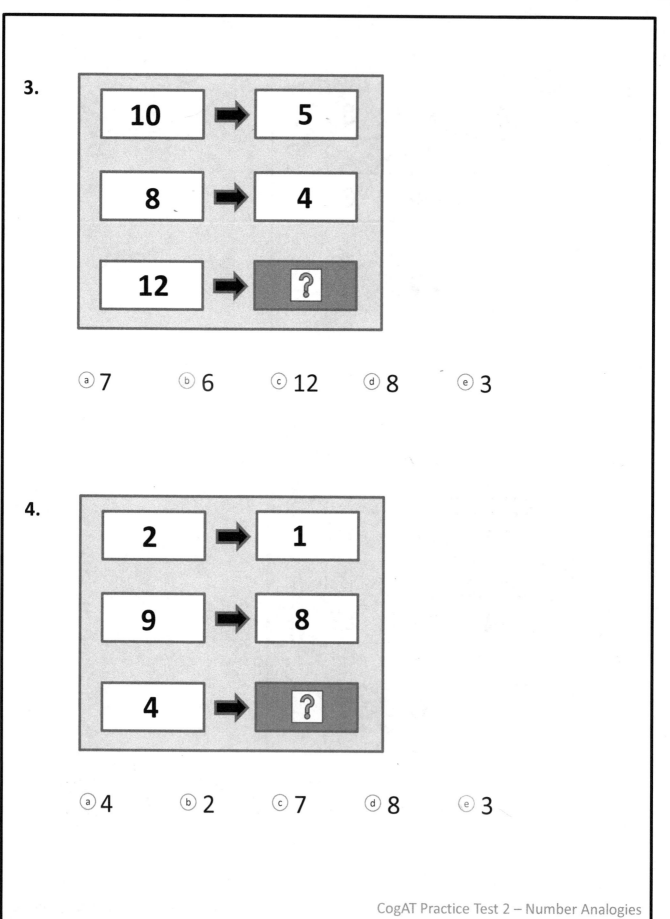

3.

10	➡	5
8	➡	4
12	➡	?

ⓐ 7　　　ⓑ 6　　　ⓒ 12　　　ⓓ 8　　　ⓔ 3

4.

2	➡	1
9	➡	8
4	➡	?

ⓐ 4　　　ⓑ 2　　　ⓒ 7　　　ⓓ 8　　　ⓔ 3

5.

3 →	**3**
2 →	**2**
1 →	**?**

ⓐ 1   ⓑ 3   ⓒ 2   ⓓ 11   ⓔ 12

6.

7 →	**12**
13 →	**18**
21 →	**?**

ⓐ 28   ⓑ 27   ⓒ 26   ⓓ 24   ⓔ 29

7.

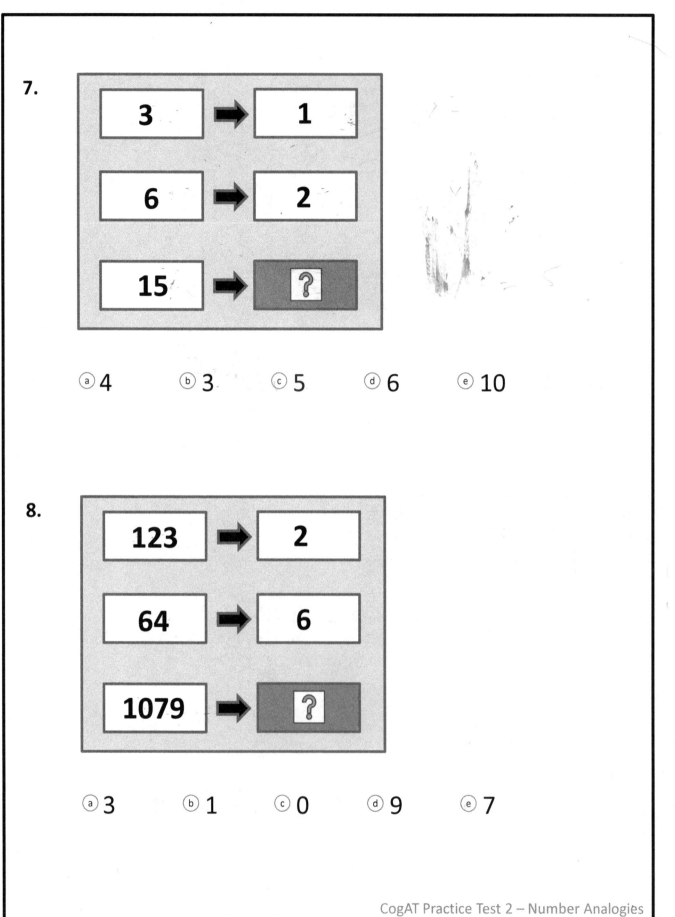

3 ➡	**1**
6 ➡	**2**
15 ➡	**?**

ⓐ 4　　ⓑ 3　　ⓒ 5　　ⓓ 6　　ⓔ 10

8.

123 ➡	**2**
64 ➡	**6**
1079 ➡	**?**

ⓐ 3　　ⓑ 1　　ⓒ 0　　ⓓ 9　　ⓔ 7

9.

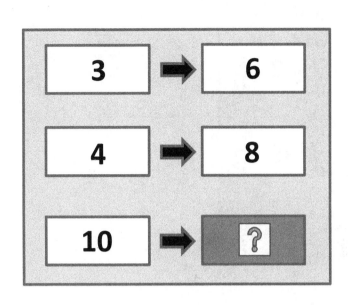

ⓐ 14   ⓑ 12   ⓒ 18   ⓓ 20   ⓔ 13

10.

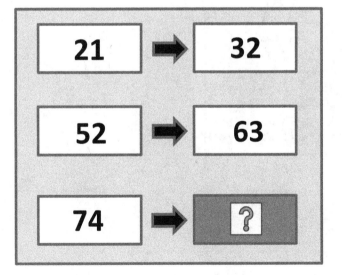

ⓐ 114   ⓑ 63   ⓒ 86   ⓓ 73   ⓔ 85

11.

7:30 ➡	7:40
7:40 ➡	7:50
7:50 ➡	?

ⓐ 8:00   ⓑ 8:10   ⓒ 7:60   ⓓ 7:70   ⓔ 6:70

12.

7 ➡	7/2
5 ➡	5/2
3 ➡	?

ⓐ 3   ⓑ 2   ⓒ 3/2   ⓓ 2/3   ⓔ 1/2

13.

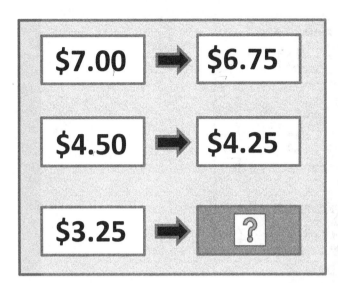

ⓐ $3.75　ⓑ $3.30　ⓒ $3.15　ⓓ $3.50　ⓔ $3.00

14.

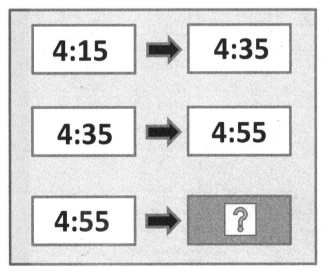

ⓐ 4:75　ⓑ 5:15　ⓒ 4:70　ⓓ 5:20　ⓔ 4:80

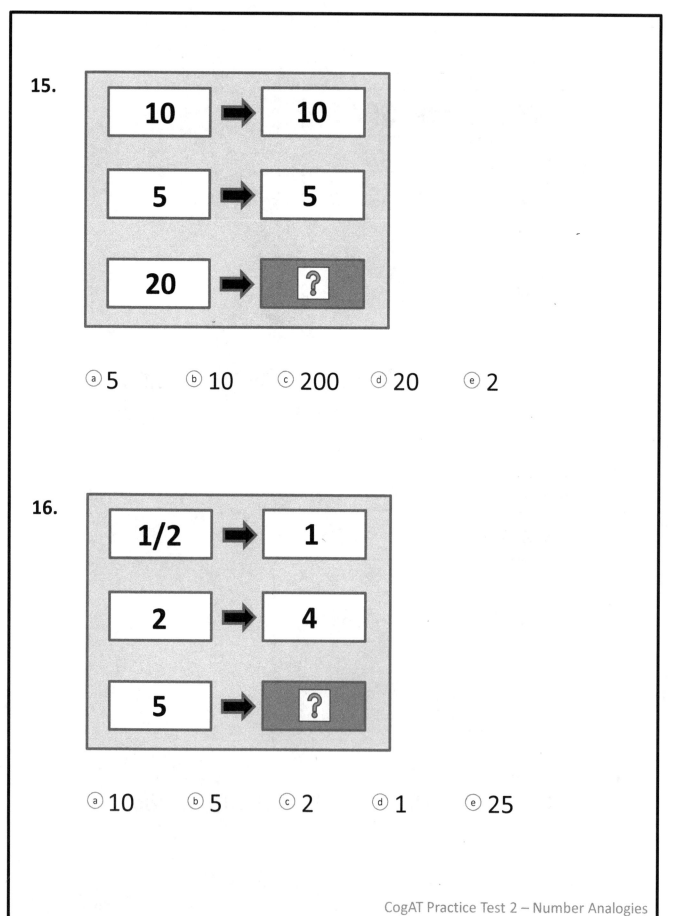

15.

10 ➡ 10

5 ➡ 5

20 ➡ ?

(a) 5   (b) 10   (c) 200   (d) 20   (e) 2

16.

1/2 ➡ 1

2 ➡ 4

5 ➡ ?

(a) 10   (b) 5   (c) 2   (d) 1   (e) 25

17.

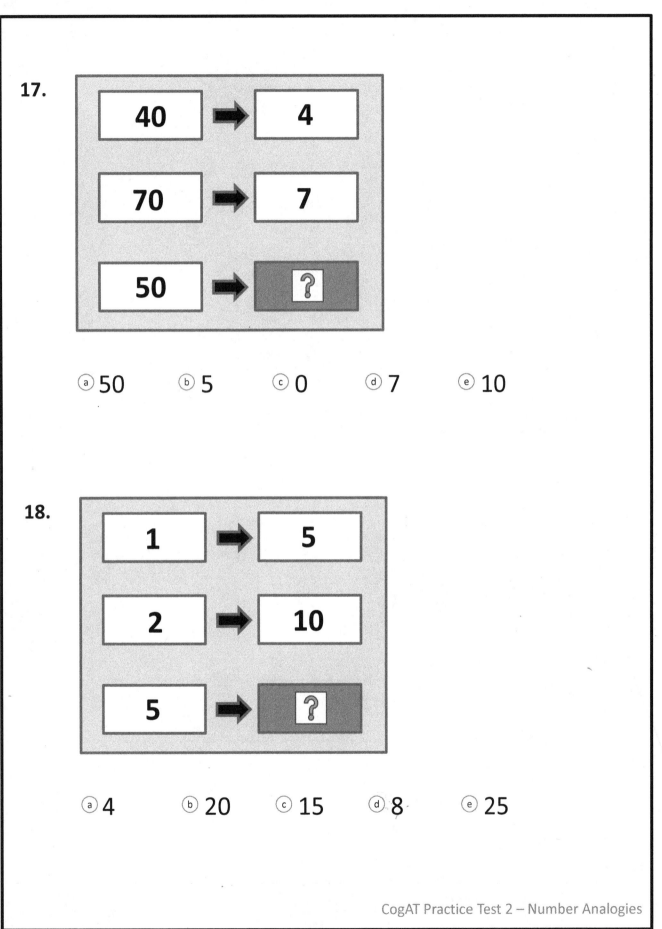

40 ➡ 4

70 ➡ 7

50 ➡ ?

  ⓐ 50   ⓑ 5   ⓒ 0   ⓓ 7   ⓔ 10

18.

1 ➡ 5

2 ➡ 10

5 ➡ ?

  ⓐ 4   ⓑ 20   ⓒ 15   ⓓ 8   ⓔ 25

NUMBER PUZZLES

In each question, find the number that will replace the question mark. Color the bubble under your choice.

1. $\boxed{?}$ = 7 + 4 + 3

    ⓐ 15   ⓑ 14   ⓒ 13   ⓓ 7   ⓔ 11

2. 20 - 5 = $\boxed{?}$

    ⓐ 12   ⓑ 15   ⓒ 10   ⓓ 11   ⓔ 25

3. $\boxed{?}$ = 2 + 7 + 5 - 4

    ⓐ 10   ⓑ 11   ⓒ 12   ⓓ 16   ⓔ 9

4. 21 = 19 + 5 - $\boxed{?}$

    ⓐ 3   ⓑ 4   ⓒ 24   ⓓ 23   ⓔ 45

5. $8 + \boxed{?} = 2 + 2 + 2 + 2$

    ⓐ 12   ⓑ 16   ⓒ 4   ⓓ 0   ⓔ 8

6. $22 = 28 + 2 - 5 - 4 + \boxed{?}$

    ⓐ 20   ⓑ 3   ⓒ 1   ⓓ 21   ⓔ 2

7. $2 \times 5 = \boxed{?}$

    ⓐ 40   ⓑ 25   ⓒ 50   ⓓ 5   ⓔ 10

8. $\boxed{?} < 6 + 5 + 4$

    ⓐ 15   ⓑ 10   ⓒ 25   ⓓ 30   ⓔ 20

9. $7 + 8 = 12 + 7 - $?

ⓐ 19   ⓑ 15   ⓒ 5   ⓓ 4   ⓔ 6

10.   ? $ > 8 + 4 + 2$

ⓐ 14   ⓑ 15   ⓒ 13   ⓓ 10   ⓔ 3

11. $5 + 5 = $? $ X 5$

ⓐ 55   ⓑ 10   ⓒ 2   ⓓ 3   ⓔ 1

12. $15 + 5 - 10 - $? $ < 5$

ⓐ 0   ⓑ 5   ⓒ 3   ⓓ 10   ⓔ 1

13. 8 + 9 - 7 = ⟦?⟧ - 3

  ⓐ 17   ⓑ 13   ⓒ 3   ⓓ 10   ⓔ 11

14. 8 > 15 + 3 - ⟦?⟧

  ⓐ 10   ⓑ 5   ⓒ 0   ⓓ 3   ⓔ 15

15. 3 + 9 + ⟦?⟧ = 3 + 6 + 9

  ⓐ 10   ⓑ 12   ⓒ 6   ⓓ 18   ⓔ 9

16. ⟦?⟧ > 4 + 10 - 2 - 2

  ⓐ 100   ⓑ 2   ⓒ 5   ⓓ 0   ⓔ 10

NUMBER SERIES

The order of the numbers at the top of each question follows some type of pattern. Pick the answer choice that completes or fits into the pattern. Color the bubble next to your choice.

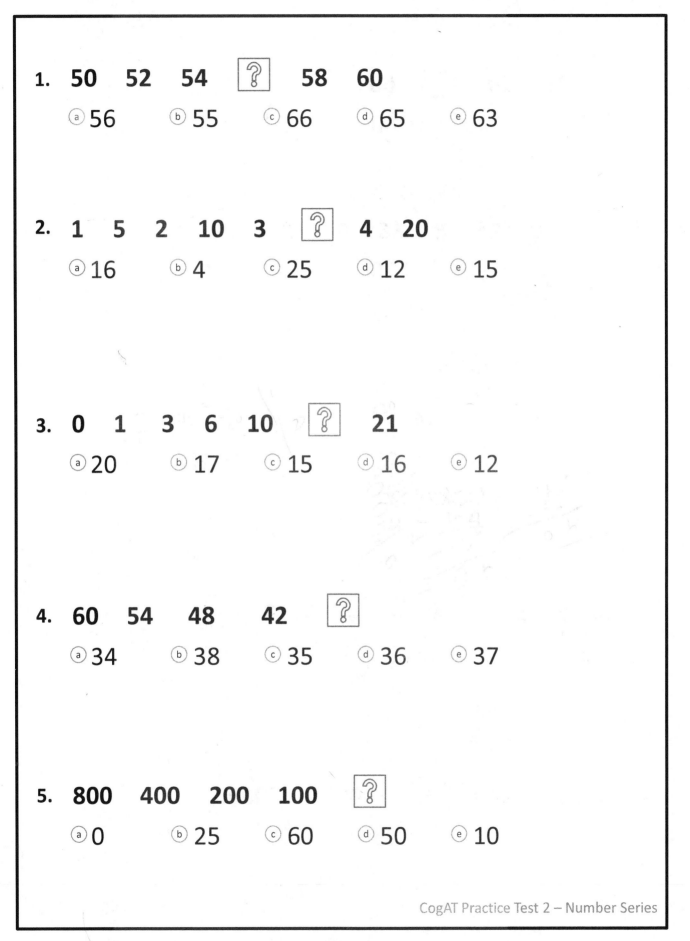

1. **50** **52** **54** [?] **58** **60**

   ⓐ 56   ⓑ 55   ⓒ 66   ⓓ 65   ⓔ 63

2. **1** **5** **2** **10** **3** [?] **4** **20**

   ⓐ 16   ⓑ 4   ⓒ 25   ⓓ 12   ⓔ 15

3. **0** **1** **3** **6** **10** [?] **21**

   ⓐ 20   ⓑ 17   ⓒ 15   ⓓ 16   ⓔ 12

4. **60** **54** **48** **42** [?]

   ⓐ 34   ⓑ 38   ⓒ 35   ⓓ 36   ⓔ 37

5. **800** **400** **200** **100** [?]

   ⓐ 0   ⓑ 25   ⓒ 60   ⓓ 50   ⓔ 10

6. **0   15   30   [?]   60**

   ⓐ 55   ⓑ 45   ⓒ 40   ⓓ 50   ⓔ 35

7. **12   10   14   8   16   6   18   [?]**

   ⓐ 4   ⓑ 6   ⓒ 20   ⓓ 16   ⓔ 9

8. **35   28   [?]   14   7**

   ⓐ 19   ⓑ 29   ⓒ 22   ⓓ 21   ⓔ 20

9. **5   5   5   5   4   4   4   3   3   [?]**

   ⓐ 3   ⓑ 1   ⓒ 5   ⓓ 5   ⓔ 2

10. **1   10   100   [?]   10000   100000**

   ⓐ 1000   ⓑ 0   ⓒ 200   ⓓ 100   ⓔ 10000

11. **20** **40** **60** 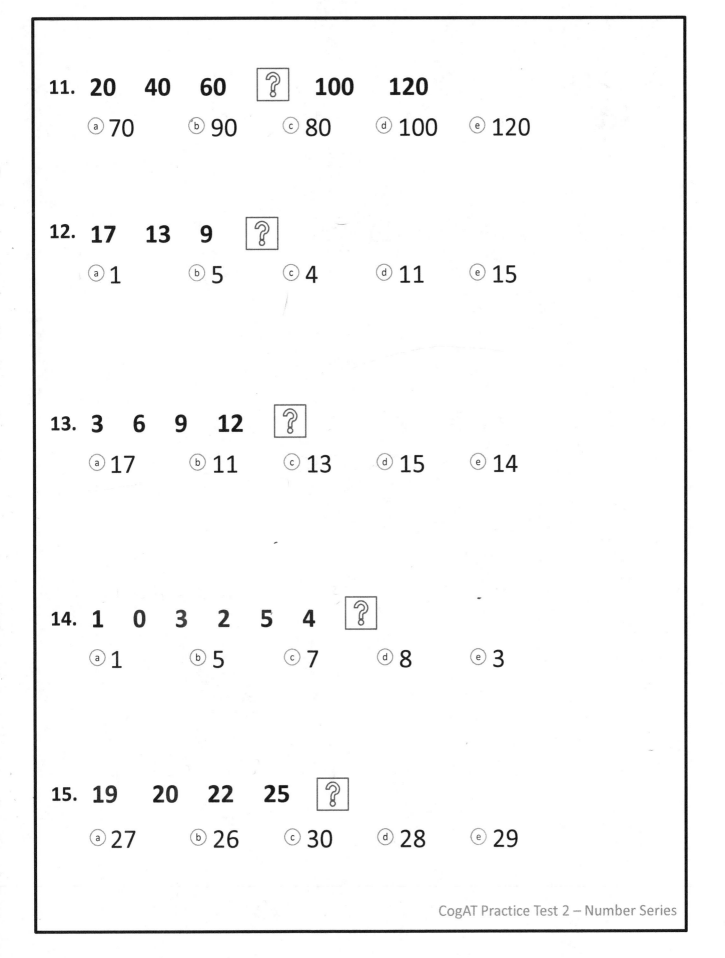 **100** **120**

    ⓐ 70   ⓑ 90   ⓒ 80   ⓓ 100   ⓔ 120

12. **17** **13** **9**

    ⓐ 1   ⓑ 5   ⓒ 4   ⓓ 11   ⓔ 15

13. **3** **6** **9** **12**

    ⓐ 17   ⓑ 11   ⓒ 13   ⓓ 15   ⓔ 14

14. **1** **0** **3** **2** **5** **4**

    ⓐ 1   ⓑ 5   ⓒ 7   ⓓ 8   ⓔ 3

15. **19** **20** **22** **25**

    ⓐ 27   ⓑ 26   ⓒ 30   ⓓ 28   ⓔ 29

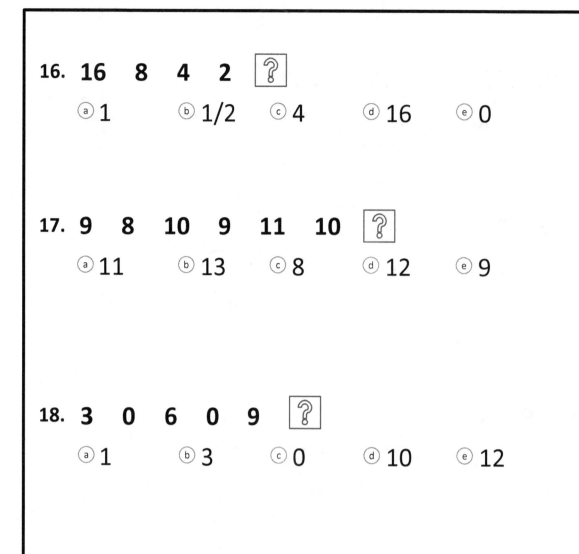

16. **16   8   4   2** [?]

ⓐ 1   ⓑ 1/2   ⓒ 4   ⓓ 16   ⓔ 0

17. **9   8   10   9   11   10** [?]

ⓐ 11   ⓑ 13   ⓒ 8   ⓓ 12   ⓔ 9

18. **3   0   6   0   9** [?]

ⓐ 1   ⓑ 3   ⓒ 0   ⓓ 10   ⓔ 12

FIGURE MATRICES

In each question, the figures follow some type of pattern. Pick the answer choice that completes or fits the pattern. Color the bubble next to your choice.

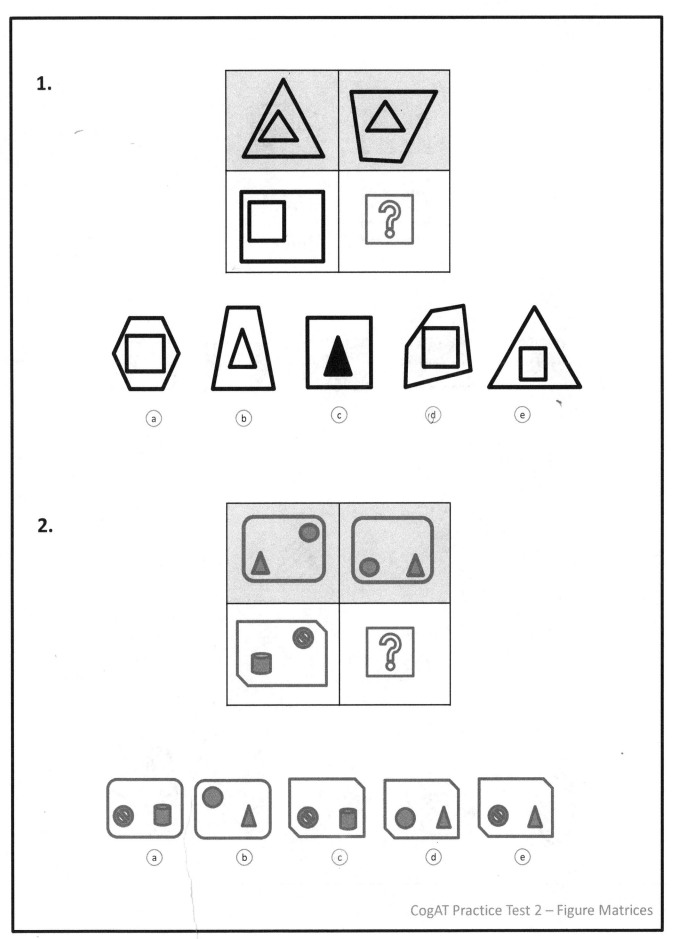

1.

2.

3.

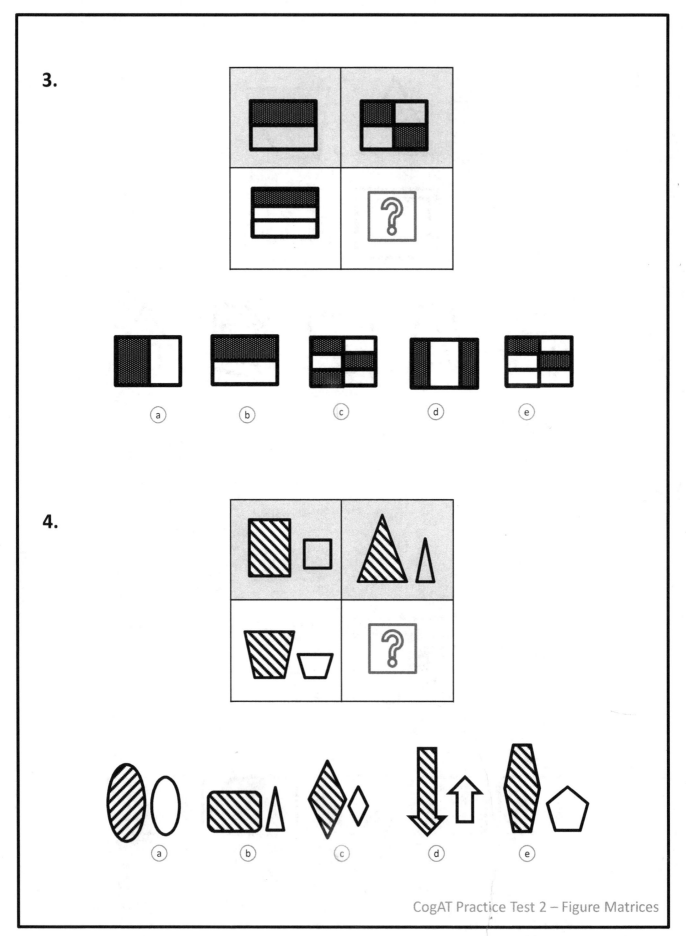

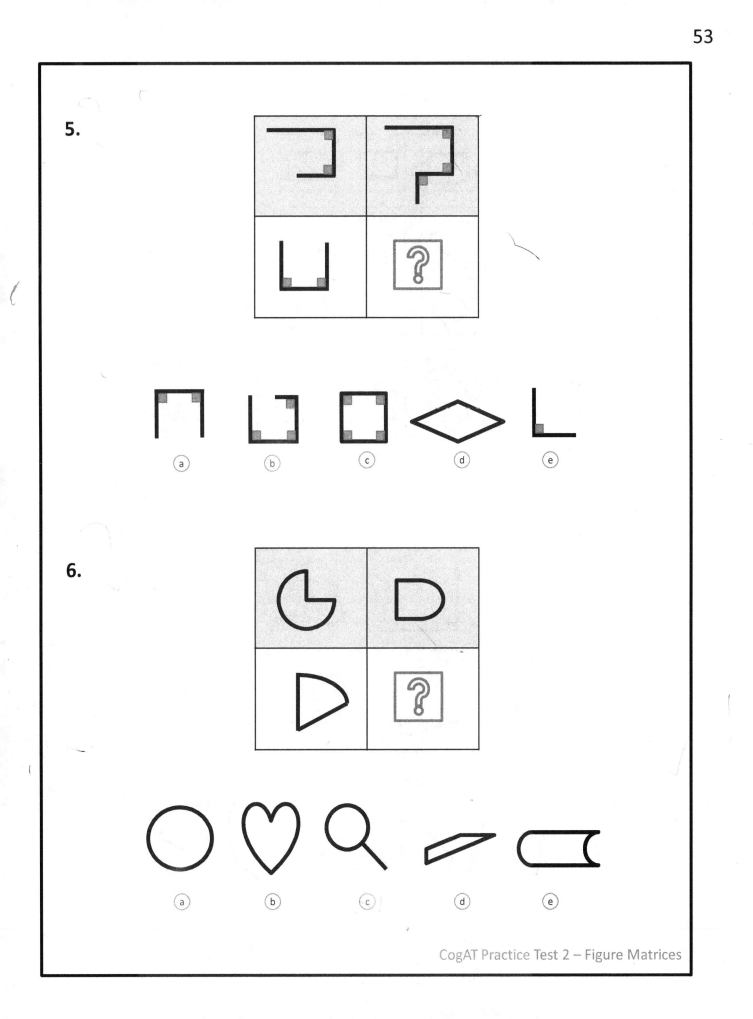

5.

6.

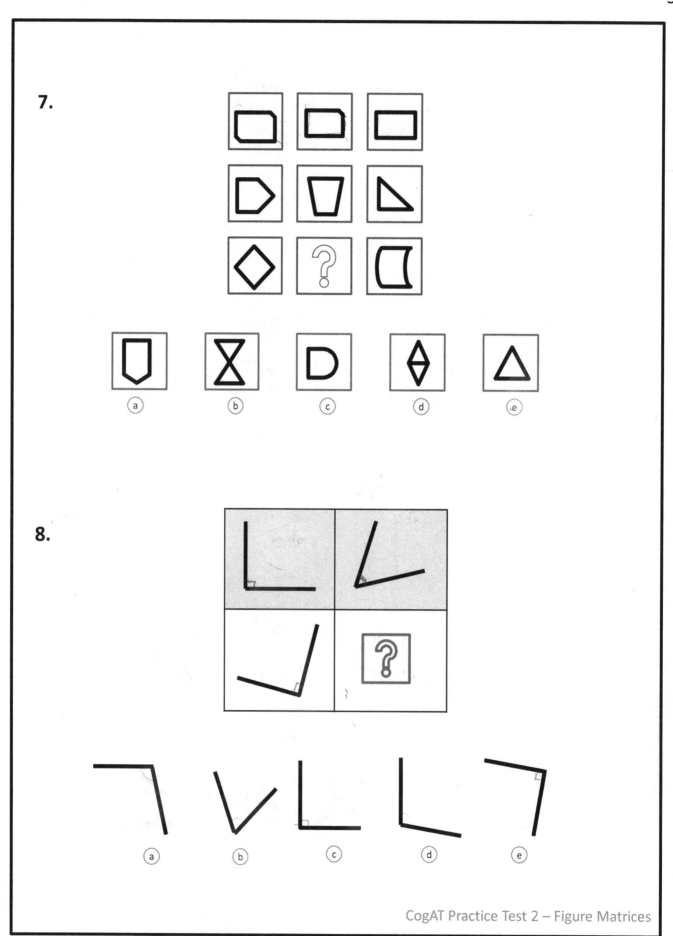

7.

a b c d e

8.

a b c d e

9.

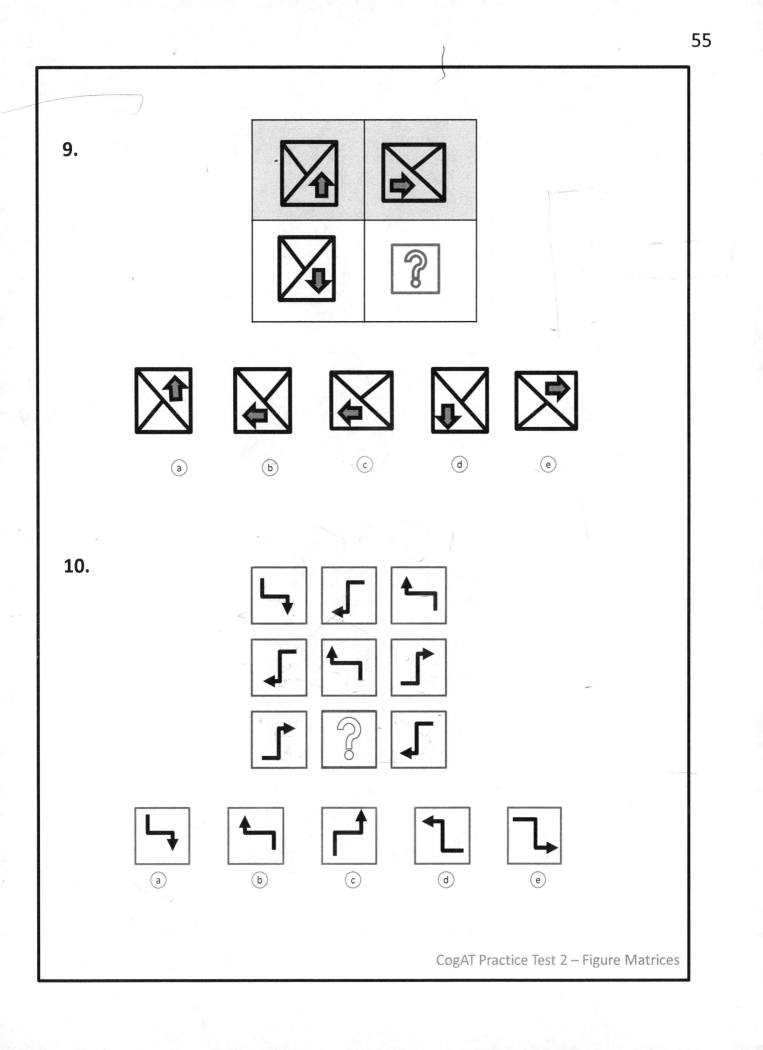

11.

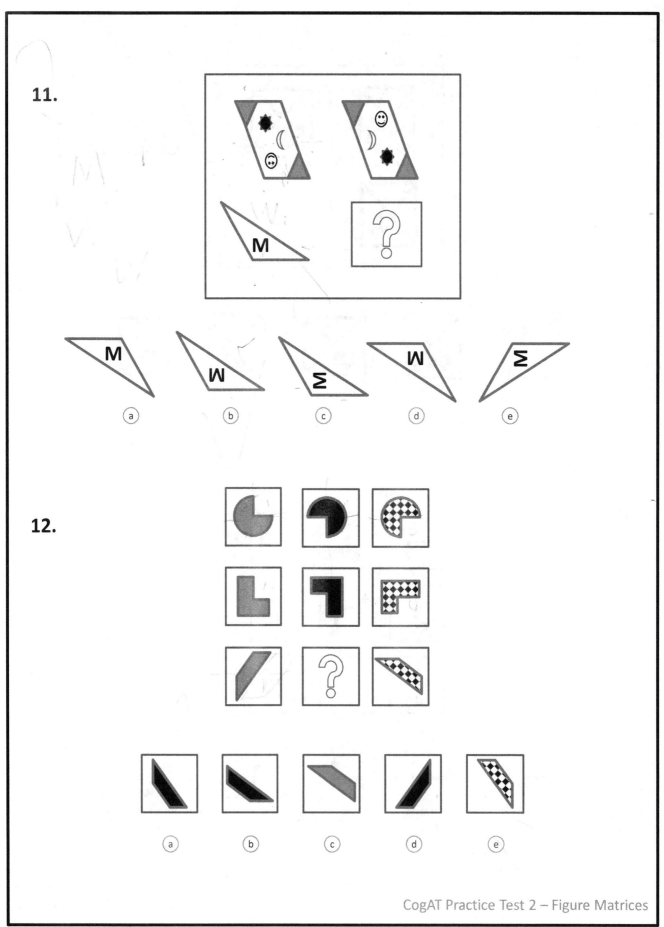

12.

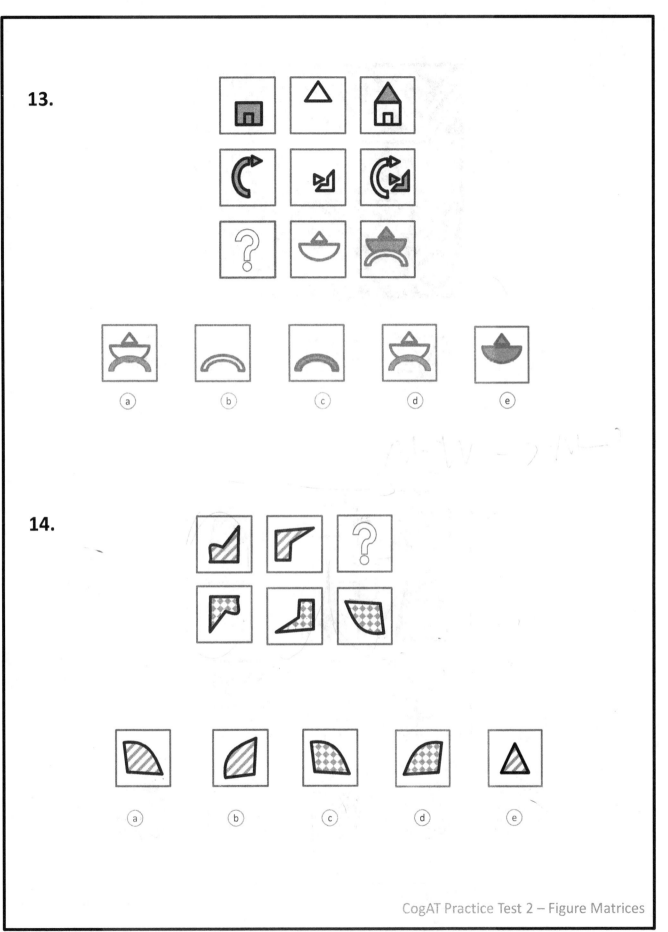

13.

14.

CogAT Practice Test 2 – Figure Matrices

15.

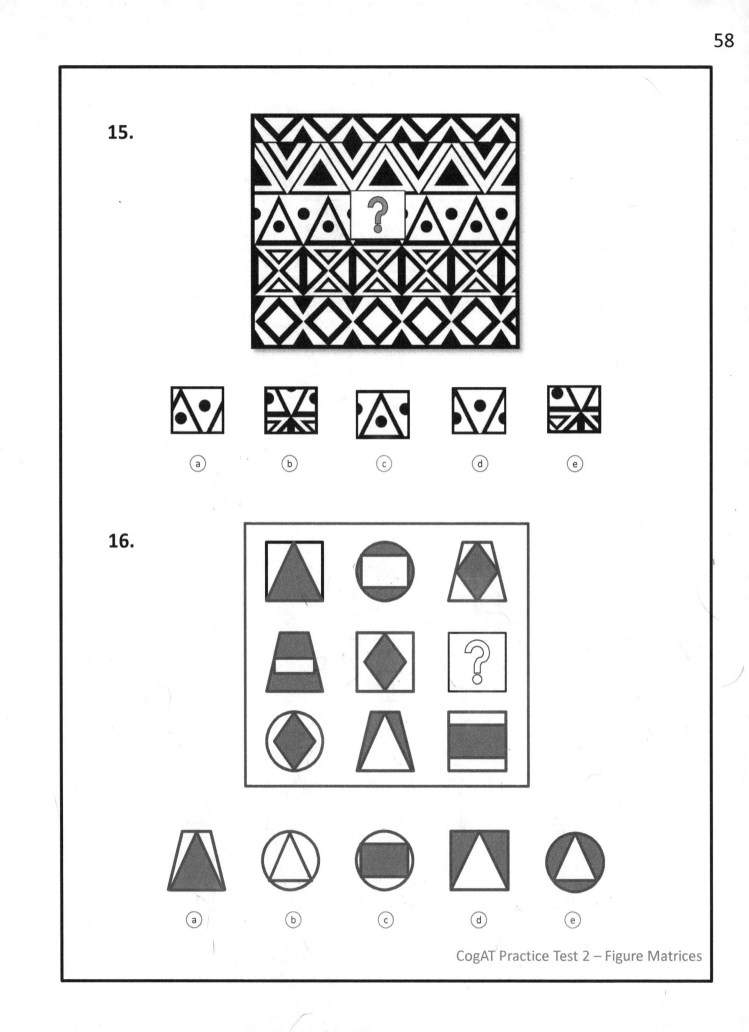

16.

17.

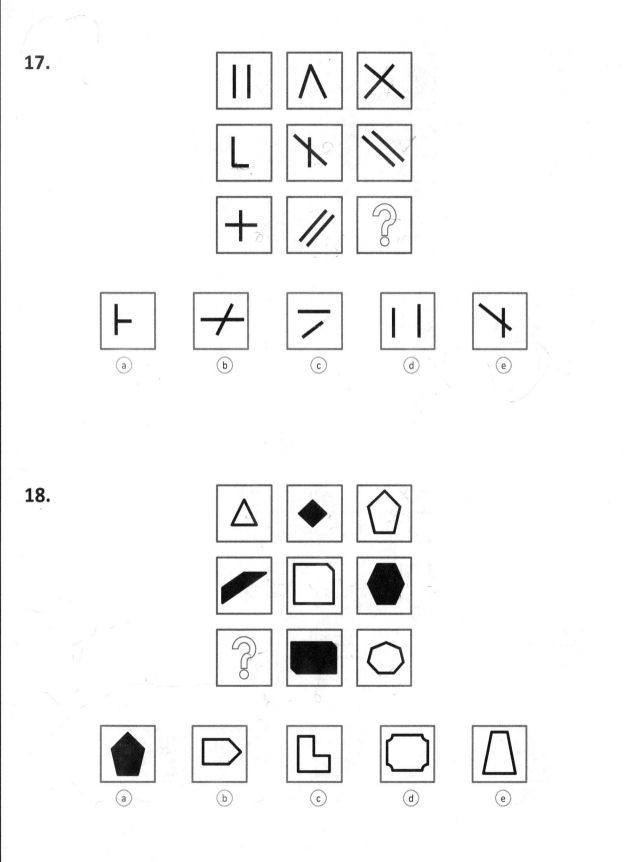

18.

19.

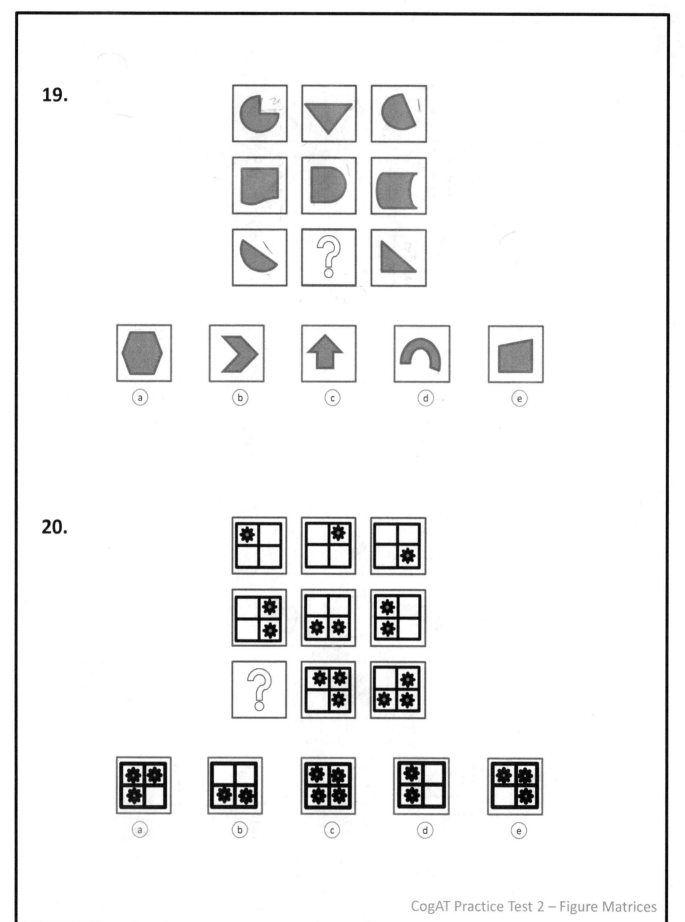

20.

PAPER FOLDING

Each question shows a piece of paper that has been folded along the line shown and then has been cut with a pair of scissors or has had holes punched through it.

Pick the answer choice that shows how the paper will look when it is unfolded. Color the bubble under your choice.

1.

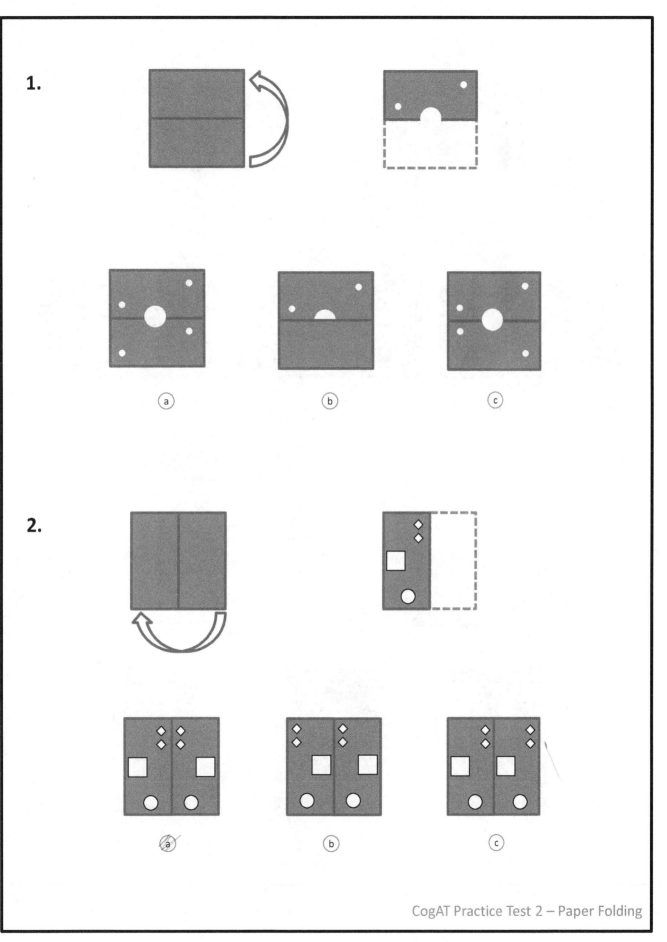

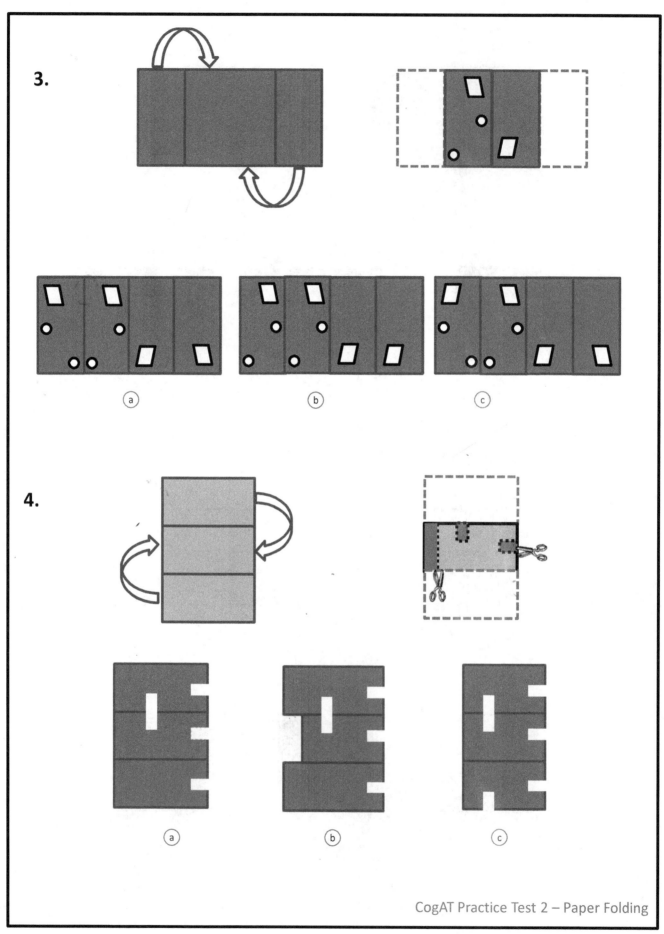

3.

    (a)   (b)   (c)

4.

    (a)   (b)   (c)

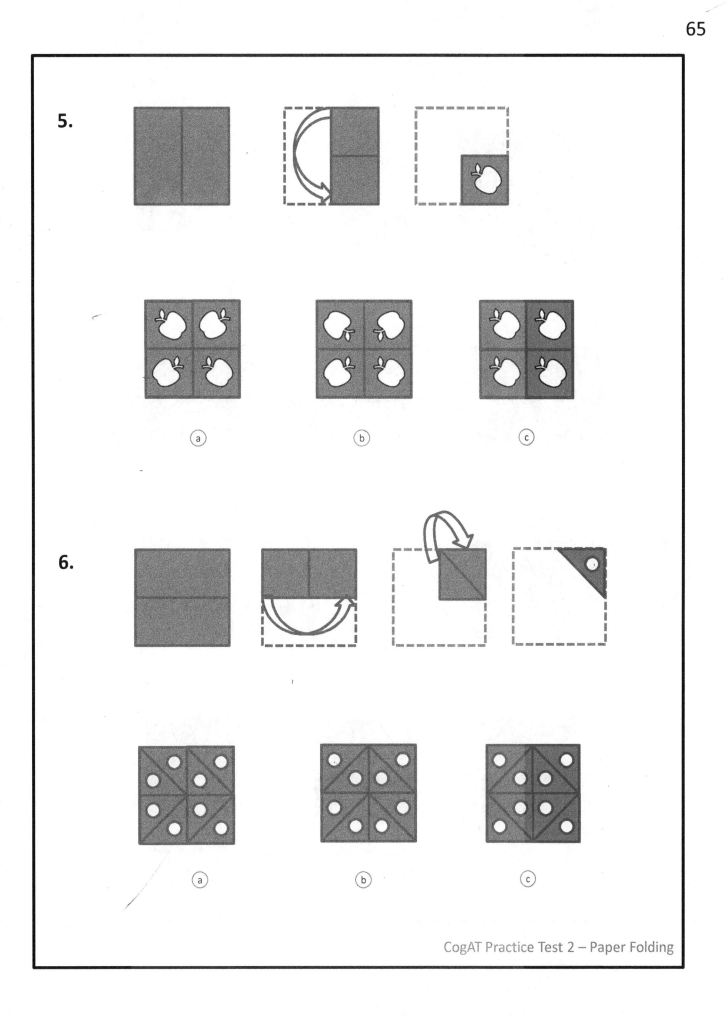

7.

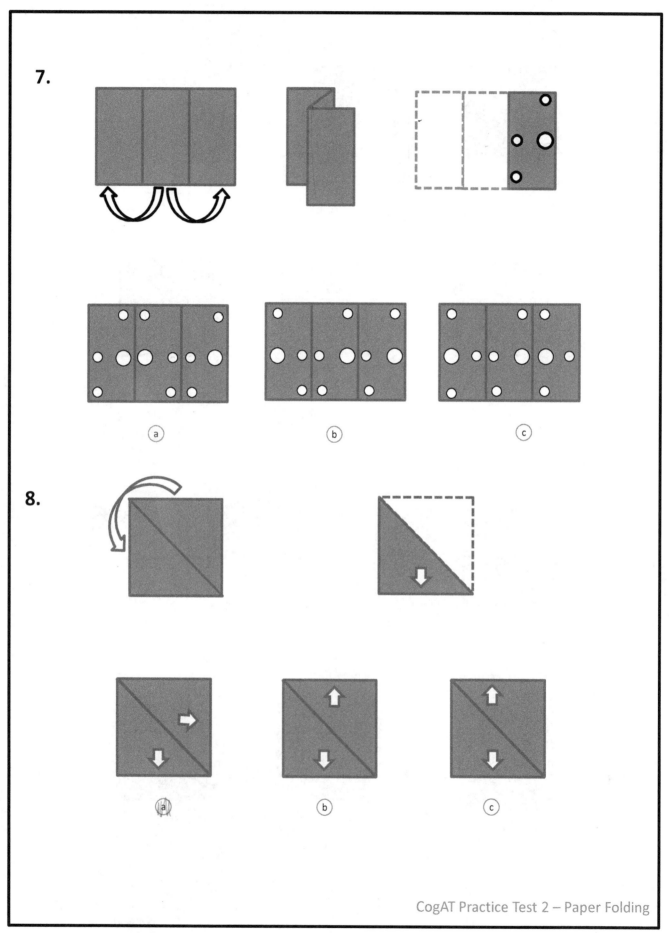

9.

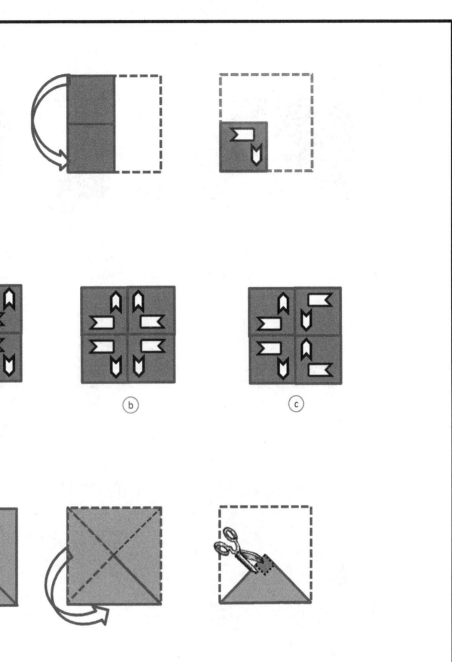

10.

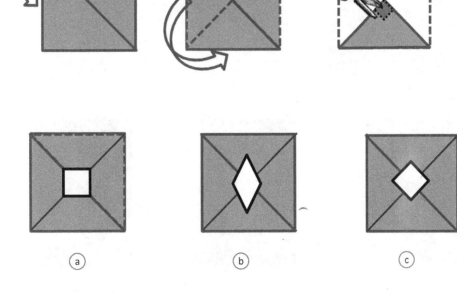

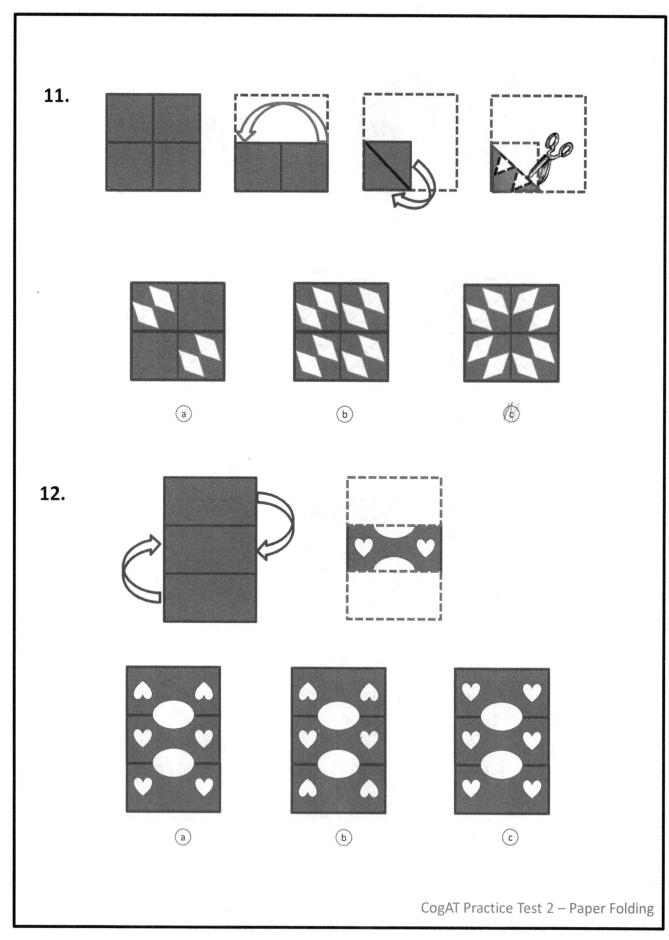

11.

(a) (b) (c)

12.

(a) (b) (c)

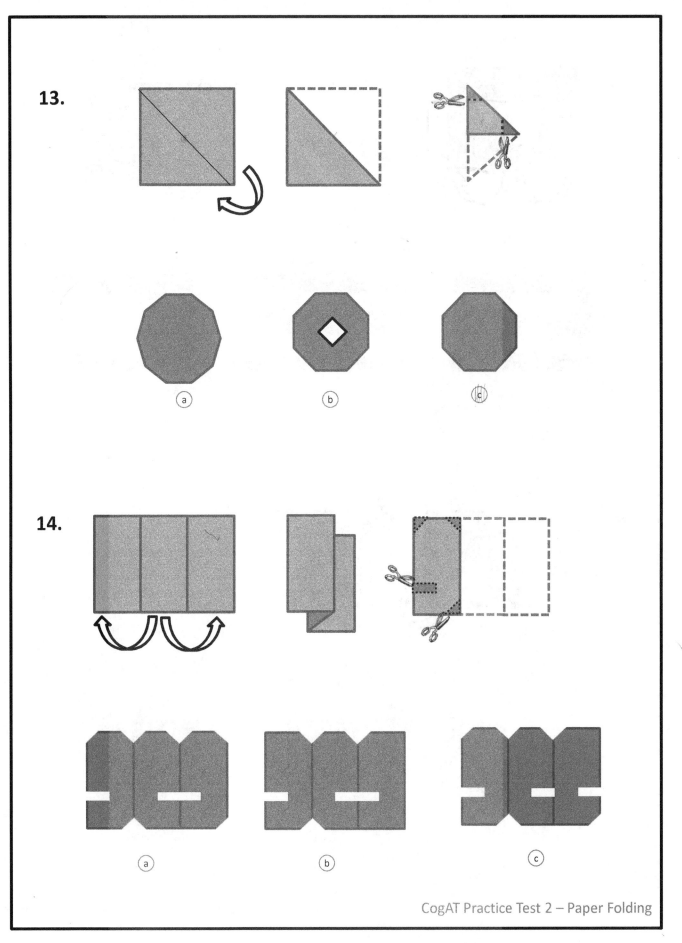

13.

14.

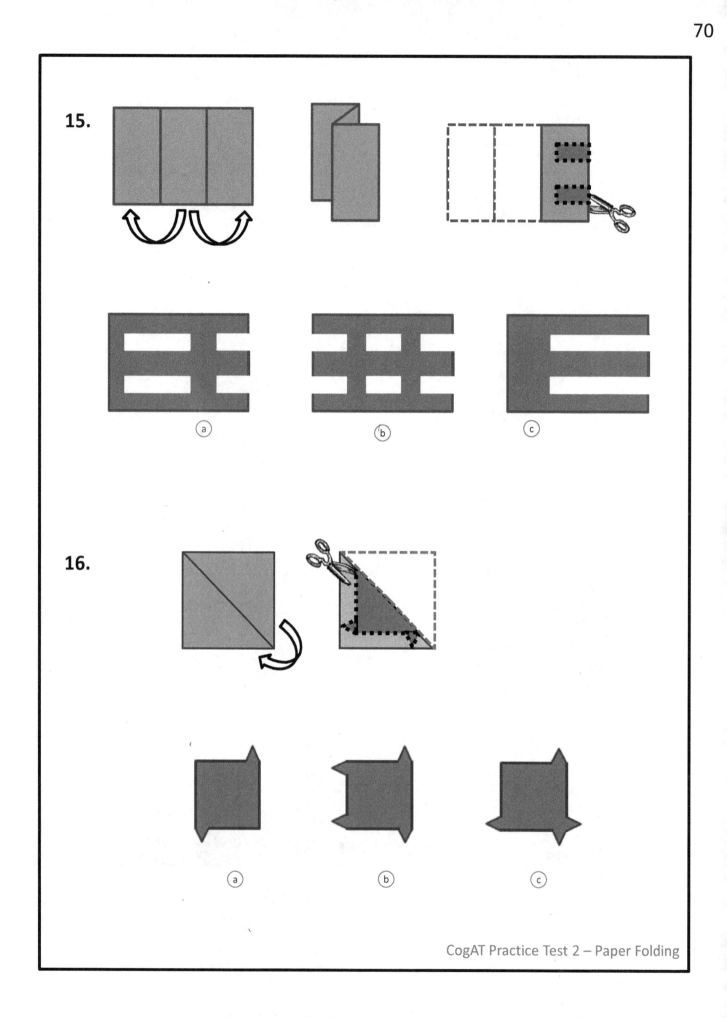

FIGURE CLASSIFICATION

Look at the top 3 pictures and determine how they are similar.

In the bottom row, color the bubble under the picture that is most similar to the top 3.

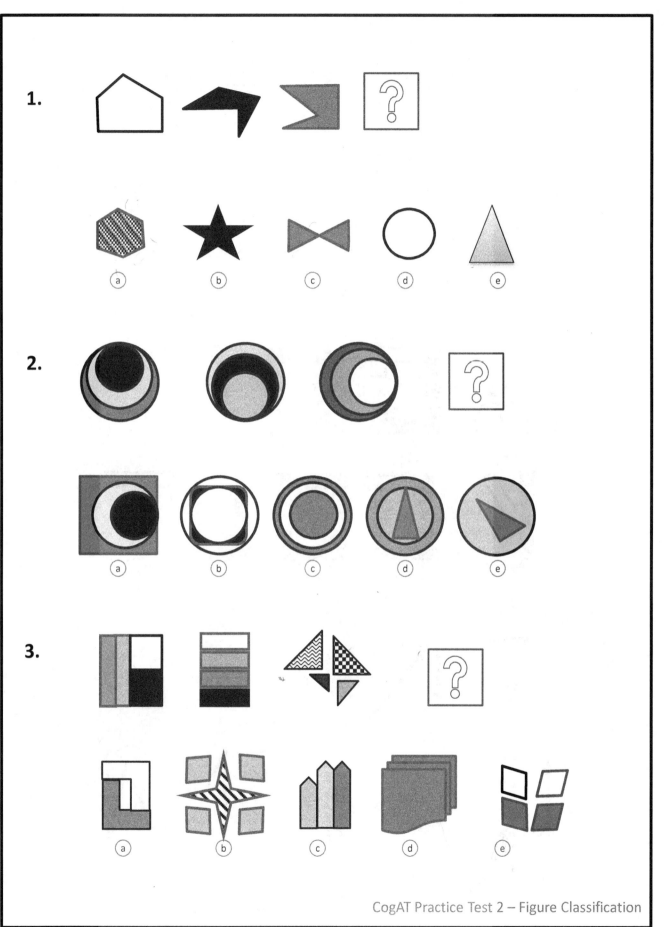

1.

2.

3.

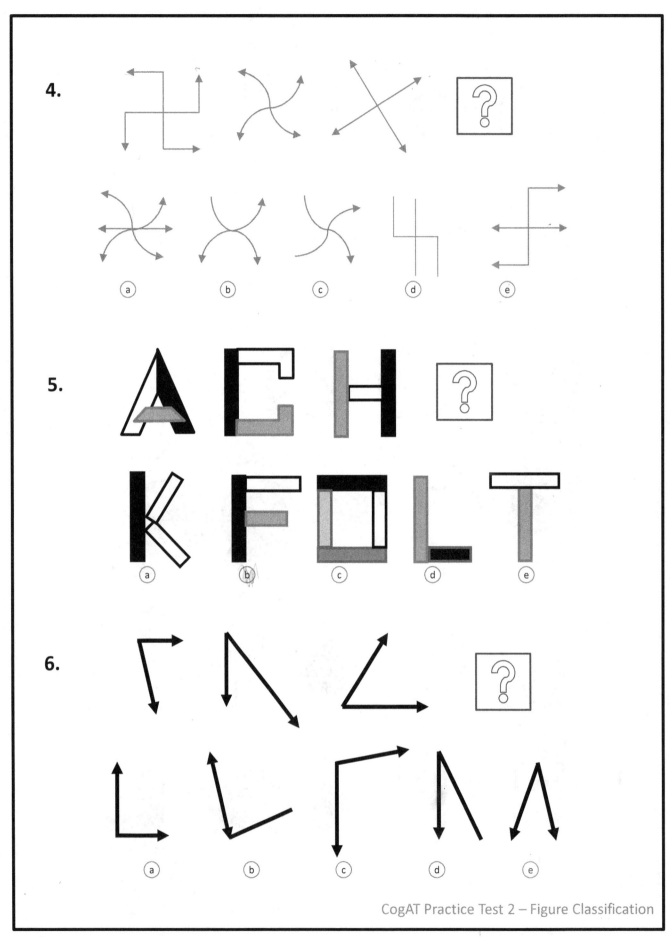

4.

    (a)   (b)   (c)   (d)   (e)

5.

    (a)   (b)   (c)   (d)   (e)

6.

    (a)   (b)   (c)   (d)   (e)

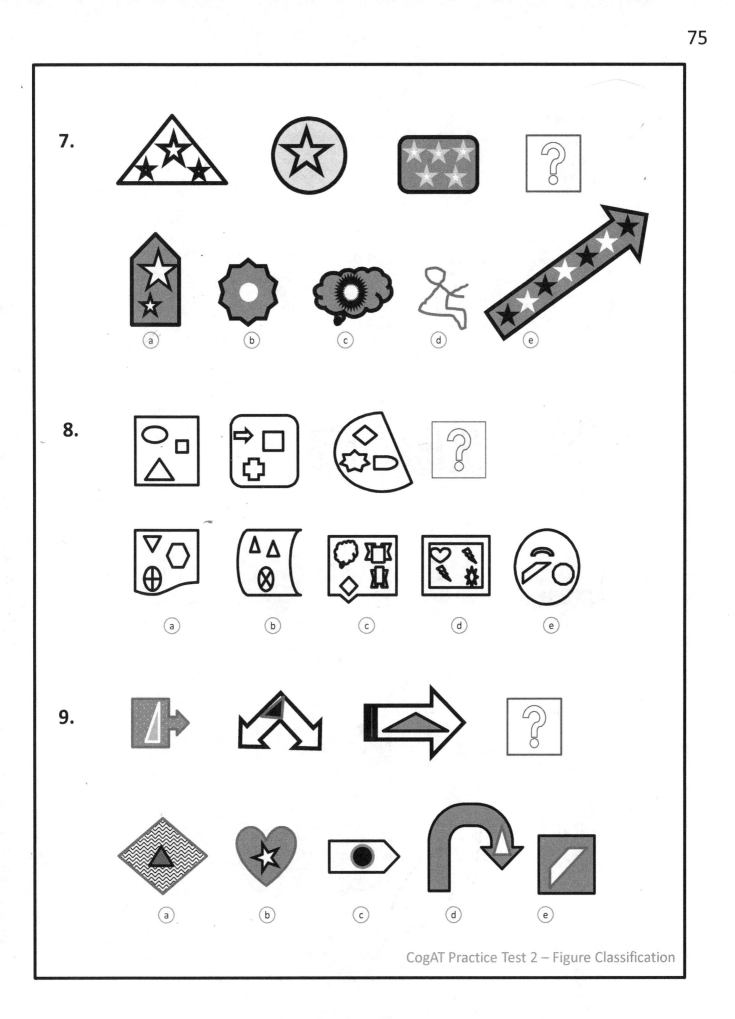

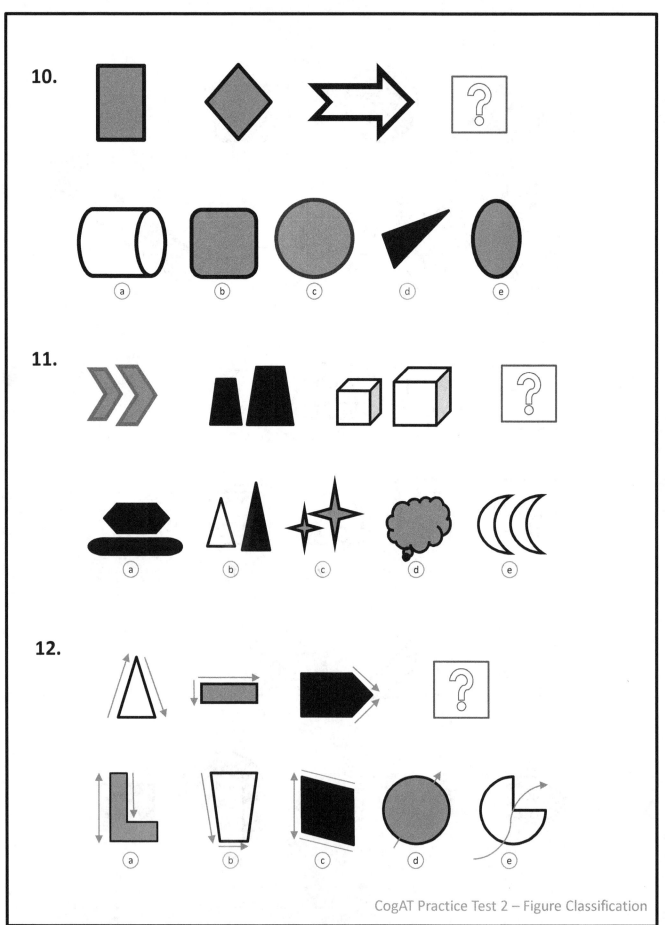

10.

11.

12.

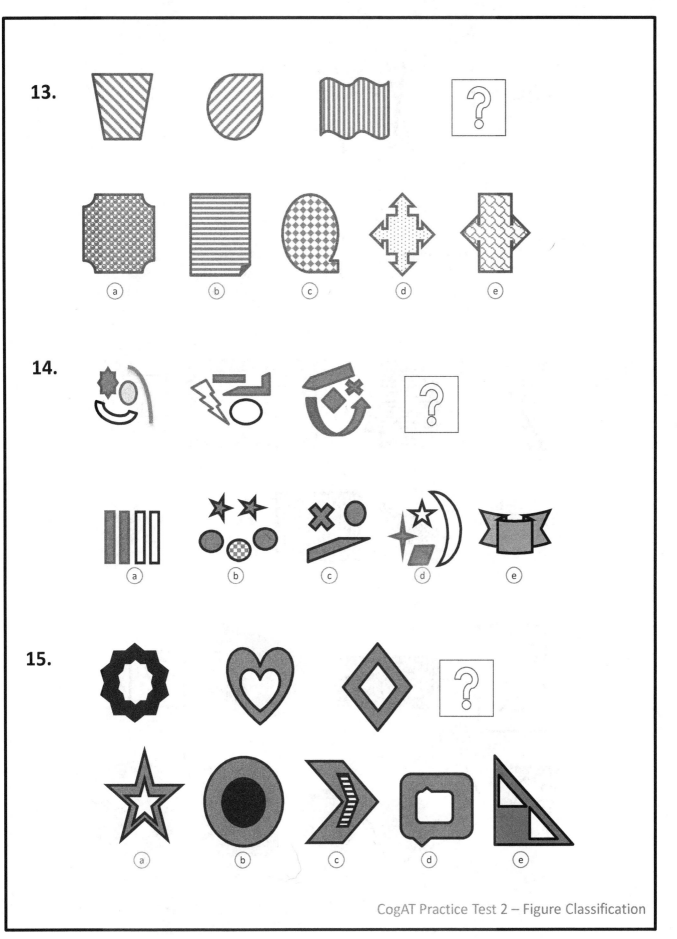

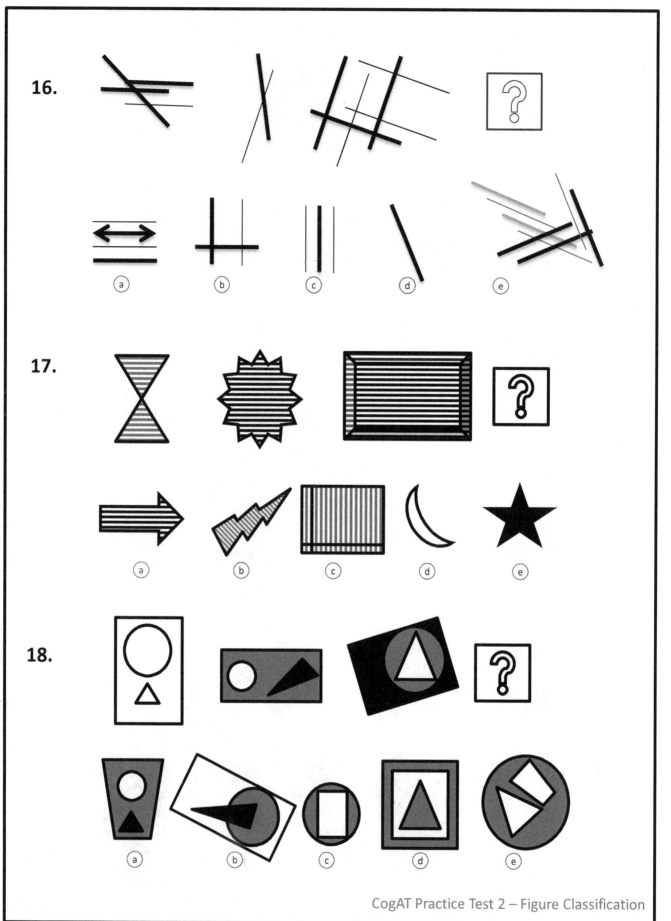

16.

17.

18.

19.

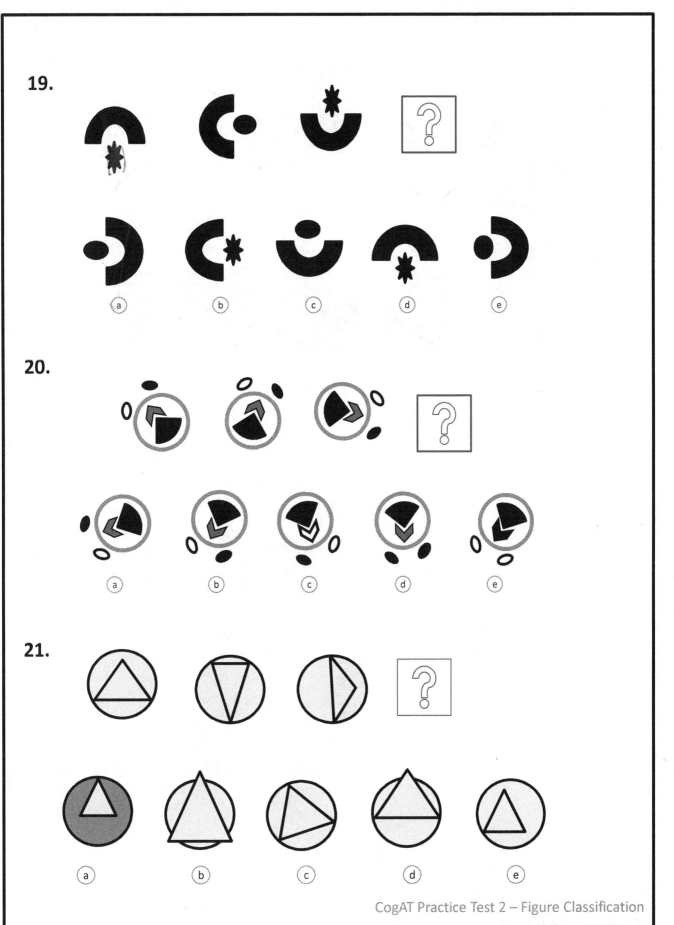

20.

21.

22.

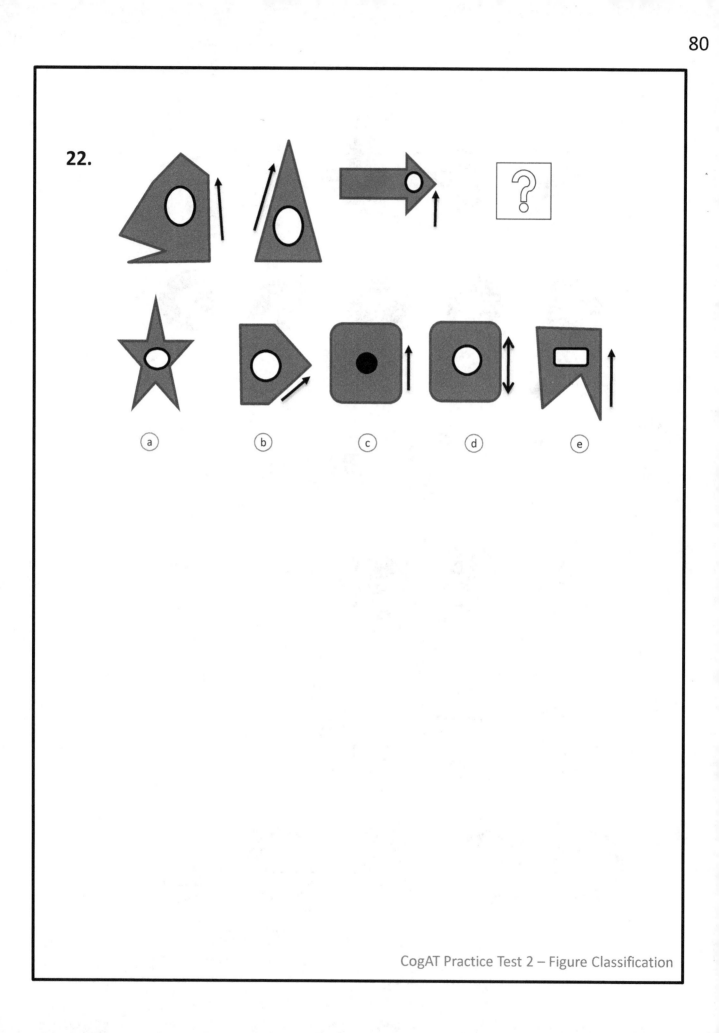

ANSWER KEY

CogAT® Practice Test 2 – ANSWER KEY

Verbal Analogies – *Pg.5 to Pg.11*

1. b

   A plant grows from a seed. A flower grows from a bud.

2. a

   Summer is the name of a season. December is the name of a month.

3. b

   Bread is made with dough. Pancakes are made with batter.

4. a

   Bees live in hives. Rabbits live in burrows.

5. c

   Coffee is made from coffee beans. Tea is made from tea leaves.

6. a

   An ocean is a body of water. Woods is a collection of trees.

7. b

   Wind moves a sailboat. Oars move a rowboat.

8. e

   A flash is a part of a camera. A mouse is part of a computer.

9. b

   A referee regulates a football match. An umpire regulates a baseball match.

10. b

    A square has four sides. A pentagon has five sides.

CogAT® Practice Test 2 – ANSWER KEY

Verbal Analogies – *Pg.5 to Pg.11*

11. b

A snake slithers. A lion prowls.

12. c

A pilot controls a plane. A captain controls a ship.

13. d

The outer covering of a nut is a shell. The outer covering of a pea is a pod.

14. c

The past tense of 'run' is 'ran'. The past tense of 'sink' is 'sank'.

15. a

A belt is worn around the waist. A bracelet is worn around the wrist.

16. d

Floods happen because of heavy rainfall. Blizzards happen because of heavy snowfall.

17. c

A teacher teaches. A doctor treats.

18. b

A cub is a young bear. A joey is a young kangaroo.

19. a

A fern is a type of plant. An eel is a type of fish.

20. e

A group of puppies is called a litter. A group of fish is called a school.

CogAT® Practice Test 2 – ANSWER KEY

Verbal Analogies – *Pg.5 to Pg.11*

21. e

A baby cat is a kitten. A baby cow is a calf.

22. b

A scientist performs experiments . An actor performs plays.

23. a

Baseball is played on a diamond. Tennis is played on a court.

24. c

Asia is a continent. Jupiter is a planet.

CogAT® Practice Test 2 – ANSWER KEY

Sentence Completion - *Pg.13 to Pg.18*

*TIP : Remember that there may be more than one 'possible' answer. You are looking for **THE BEST** answer choice.*

1. b
2. b
3. a
4. e
5. c
6. c
7. e
8. b
9. b
10. a

11. e
12. d
13. b
14. e
15. a
16. c
17. e
18. d
19. c
20. e

CogAT® Practice Test 2 – ANSWER KEY

Verbal Classification – *Pg.19 to Pg.24*

1. b
   Dairy products.

2. b
   Water transportation.

3. a
   Root vegetables.

4. e
   Animal sounds.

5. d
   Names of flowers.

6. d
   Names of Planets.

7. c
   Active verbs.

8. d
   Stationery.

9. a
   Birds of prey.

10. b
    Marine mammals.

CogAT® Practice Test 2 – ANSWER KEY

Verbal Classification – *Pg.19 to Pg.24*

11. e
   Nuts

12. b
   Animals that have horns.

13. a
   Desserts.

14. c
   Aircrafts.

15. d
   Adjectives.

16. d
   Professions.

17. d
   Freshwater bodies.

18. b
   Holidays.

19. d
   Types of jewelry.

20. d
   Outdoor sports.

CogAT® Practice Test 2 – ANSWER KEY

Number Analogies – *Pg.25 to Pg.35*

1. c
   Add four.

2. b
   Subtract two.

3. b
   Halve.

4. e
   Subtract one.

5. a
   Add or subtract zero.

6. c
   Add five.

7. c
   Divide into three equal parts.

8. e
   The number in the tens place.

9. d
   Double.

CogAT® Practice Test 2 – ANSWER KEY

Number Analogies – *Pg.25 to Pg.35*

10. e
Add eleven.

11. a
Add ten minutes.

12. c
'Divide' by two. (Looking for an intuitive answer selection)

13. e
Subtract twenty-five cents.

14. b
Add twenty minutes.

15. d
Add or subtract zero.

16. a
Double.

17. b
The number in the tens place.

18. e
Multiply by five or skip counting by five. (as in clock math)

CogAT® Practice Test 2 – ANSWER KEY

Number Puzzles – *Pg.37 to Pg.42*

1. b
    $14 = 7 + 4 + 3$

2. b
    $20 - 5 = 15$

3. a
    $10 = 2 + 7 + 5 - 4$

4. a
    $21 = 19 + 5 - 3$

5. d
    $8 + 0 = 2 + 2 + 2 + 2$

6. c
    $22 = 28 + 2 - 5 - 4 + 1$

7. e
    $2 \times 5 = 10$

8. b
    $10 < 6 + 5 + 4$

CogAT® Practice Test 2 – ANSWER KEY

Number Puzzles – *Pg.37 to Pg.42*

9. d
   $7 + 8 = 12 + 7 - 4$

10. b
    $15 > 8 + 4 + 2$

11. c
    $5 + 5 = 2 * 5$

12. d
    $15 + 5 - 10 - 10 < 5$

13. b
    $8 + 9 - 7 = 13 - 3$

14. e
    $8 > 15 + 3 - 15$

15. c
    $3 + 9 + 6 = 3 + 6 + 9$

16. a
    $100 > 4 + 10 - 2 - 2$

CogAT® Practice Test 2 – ANSWER KEY

Number Series – *Pg.43 to Pg.48*

1. a
Add two.

2. e
In each number pair, the second number is five times the first. (Skip counting by five.)

3. c
Number pattern formed by starting with zero and adding one, two, three etc progressively .

4. d
Subtract six.

5. d
Halve.

6. b
Add fifteen.

7. a
Alternate numbers starting with the first number, increase by two. Alternate numbers starting with the second number decrease by two.

8. d
Subtract seven.

9. e
Each number is repeated one less number of time as the value of the number.

CogAT® Practice Test 2 – ANSWER KEY

Number Series – *Pg.43 to Pg.48*

10. a
Multiply by ten. (Add another zero at the end of each number in the sequence) .

11. c
Add twenty.

12. b
Subtract four.

13. d
Add three.

14. c
Subtract one ; Add three.

15. e
Number pattern formed by adding one, two, three etc   progressively .

16. a
Half of the previous number.

17. d
Subtract one ; Add two.

18. c
Alternate numbers starting with the first number, increase by three. Alternate numbers starting with the second number remain zero.

CogAT® Practice Test 2 – ANSWER KEY

Figure Matrices – *Pg.49 to Pg.60*

1. **d**

   Inner shape remains the same. Outer shape's number of sides/corner increases by one. No change in color.

2. **c**

   Outer shape remains the same. Mimic the position change of the inner shapes.

3. **e**

   The same fraction of the shape is colored/shaded.

4. **c**

   Two similar shapes. Larger is shaded ; smaller is white. Shading is with downward diagonal lines.

5. **b**

   Increase in the number of right angles from two to three.

6. **c**

   Figure with two straight lines and one curved line transforms into figure with one straight line and one curved line.

7. **e**

   Each column has one less straight side than the previous.

8. **b**

   Right angle becomes acute angle.
   Tip : Students are not expected to know the terminology but just a visual observation of the different angle sizes.

9. **c**

   90 degree rotation to the right. (clockwise)

10. **a**

    The movement across the columns is a 90 degree rotation to the right. (clockwise)

CogAT® Practice Test 2 – ANSWER KEY

Figure Matrices – *Pg.49 to Pg.60*

11. d

180 degree rotation to the right. (clockwise)

12. d

The second column is a 180 degree rotation of the first column with a change in color.

13. c

Merge figures in column one and column two and swap colors to get column three.

14. a

The top row is a 180 degree rotation of the bottom row with a different fill pattern.

15. c

Tip : Slash the Trash!

16. e

Each row/column should have a set of the three different images with a combination of six different shapes. Also note the color swap across the rows.

17. a

Each row/column is made with a two sticks placed in three different patterns (Parallel / touching / intersecting).

18. b

The movement across rows/column shows the number of sides in the figure increasing by one. The colors swap from black to white as well.

19. d

Each row/column is made of figures with 1,2 and 3 straight sides.

20. a

The movement across the rows from L-R is a 90 degree rotation to the left. (Counter clockwise)

CogAT® Practice Test 2 – ANSWER KEY

Paper Folding – *Pg.61 to Pg.70*

1. c
2. a
3. c
4. c
5. b
6. c
7. a
8. a
9. b
10. c
11. c
12. b
13. c
14. a
15. a
16. c

CogAT® Practice Test 2 – ANSWER KEY

Figure Classification – *Pg.71 to Pg.80*

1. c
    A figure with five corners.

2. c
    A figure with three concentric circles.

3. e
    An image comprised of four individual shapes.

4. e
    An image comprised of four individual arrows.

5. b
    An alphabet made up of 3 rectangles that are each of a different color.

6. e
    An acute angle made with two single headed arrows.

7. e
    A figure with an odd number of stars inside it.

8. e
    A figure with three different shapes inside it, one of which is a four sided shape.

9. d
    A figure made of a triangle inside an arrow.

10. d
    A shape with all sharp corners.

11. c
    An image comprised of two same shaped, same colored but different sized figures.

CogAT® Practice Test 2 – ANSWER KEY

Figure Classification – *Pg.71 to Pg.80*

12. b

Two single headed arrow on two of the sides of a shape.

13. b

A shape shaded with lines on the inside.

14. d

An image comprised of four dissimilar shapes.

15. a

A figure composed of two similar shapes one inside the other. The inner shape is white in color.

16. e

Even number of sticks.

17. a

A shape filled with horizontal lines.

18. b

A figure comprised of a circle and a triangle inside of a rectangle.

19. a

A sequence of counter clockwise rotation of two alternating figures.

20. a

Rotation of the same figure.

21. c

A circle with a triangle inside with at least two points of the triangle touching the circumference of the circle.

22. b

A figure with a white circle inside it and a one sided arrow by its side.

My personal notes

I need to remember to:

I need to watch out for :

CPSIA information can be obtained
at www.ICGtesting.com
Printed in the USA
LVHW061053160719
624247LV00020B/306/P